Prof Slop

Diane Wilmer Redmond and Paul Dowling

This is the story of
Professor Sloppovichkiev.
Now, that really is quite a
mouthful so most people
just call him Prof Slop.

and mend any machine
in the universe.

But when it comes to doing
anything around the house,
well – he's a shambles!
He can't clean up, wash up,
tidy up or even put the
kettle on.
His lab is a tip and
he looks like a scarecrow.

"I'm ashamed of you!"
cries Mrs Sloppovichkiev.
"Why don't you comb your hair,
or change your clothes?"
"Tut, tut!" grumbles Prof Slop.
"You're disgusting!"
yells Mrs Sloppovichkiev.
"Oh! I can't be bothered with boring
things when I've got inventions
on my mind," answers Prof Slop.
"Then I won't come in here any more,"
says Mrs Sloppovichkiev. "Not until you tidy up!"

Prof Slop has a long, hard think, and decides that something must be done.

"I can build robots and spaceships,
make rockets that fly;
but I can't clean the house,
or help my dear wife.
It just isn't good enough,
I must do a lot more.
I know! I'll make gadgets,
I can do that for sure!"

"I'll write a **long** list
of things I can do.
I'll invent a machine
that will wash and shampoo.
I'll think of another
that will polish the floor
and tidy my lab
with gadgets galore!"

Prof Slop stays in his lab for a week.

Mrs Sloppovichkiev thinks he's in a
big sulk so she ignores him
and sulks too.

By the end of the week strange noises are coming out of the lab and Mrs Sloppovichkiev starts to worry.

First there's a tip-tapping,

then a pip-pip-popping,

followed by a beep-beeping

and a splish-splashing

and, finally, a loud clink-clanking.

"Ooh! Please open the door," begs Mrs Sloppovichkiev.
"No!" shouts Prof Slop. "Not until I've finished my work."

Two days later Prof Slop walks out of
his lab and smiles at Mrs Sloppovichkiev.
"Come in my dear," he says.
"Certainly not!" she answers.
"I've made some improvements,"
says Prof Slop. "I'm sure you'll like them."

Mrs Sloppovichkiev walks into the lab.
"Humph!" she sniffs. "It doesn't look
any different."

"Ah, but it is different," smiles the Prof as he taps the keys on his computer.

A gadget suddenly shoots out of the cupboard behind him, flings a towel around his shoulders and starts to squirt warm water onto his hair.

"Wonderful! Wonderful!" cries
Mrs Sloppovichkiev.
"Oh, that's nothing," laughs Prof Slop
and quickly types more instructions
into his computer.

Two metal arms fly out of a drawer
behind him and start to squeeze shampoo
onto his hair.

"Ow! Ow!" yells Prof Slop, "I've got soap in my eyes." He pulls a lever on his desk and a flannel on a spring pops out of the filing cabinet and gently wipes the soap off his face.

"Brilliant!" laughs Mrs Sloppovichkiev.

"Wait till you see the rest," beams Prof Slop.

"While I'm sitting here, having my hair washed I can sweep the floor and dust the furniture too."

"Rubbish!" says his wife. "Nobody can do three things at once."

"I can't," agrees the Prof, "but my gadgets can."

He taps the keys on his computer and a long rod with a brush on the end whizzes out of his cupboard. CLANK! CLANK! CLANK! goes the machine as it climbs the stairs and brushes them down.
"What next!" gasps Mrs Sloppovichkiev.
"Just watch," smiles Prof Slop.

Mrs Sloppovichkiev can't believe her eyes when the drawer beside her opens and out pops a feather duster.

"Ooh! What's that?" she asks.
"Just another little surprise," says the Prof as the duster zips around the lab, cleaning down the equipment.

In ten minutes the room is sparkling clean, spic and span.

"Bright as a new pin," says Mrs Sloppovichkiev.

"So, my dear," says Prof Slop,
"I have eye-wipers,
hair-washers,
stair-beaters,
shampoo-squeezers,
towel-flappers,
dust-raisers
and flannel-finders.
Is there anything else you want?"

"Yes, please," says Mrs Sloppovichkiev.
"I'd like a nice cup of tea."

"That's just what I thought you'd say,"
laughs Prof Slop.
He types a password into his computer
and a kettle comes whistling up
through the floorboards.
"I don't believe it!" giggles Mrs Sloppovichkiev.

A long, metal arm tips hot water into the teapot,
stirs the tea, puts the lid on,
pours out the tea then hands a
cup and saucer to Mrs Sloppovichkiev.

"Ooh! Thank you," she splutters, "thank you very much."

Mrs Sloppovichkiev gulps back her tea
and hurries away.
"I've had enough inventions for one day,"
she says.

Prof Slop closes the door behind her and smiles.
Little does she know that he's only just started!